Discipleship with Monday in Mind

(16 CHURCHES)

Connecting Faith and Work

Luke Bobo with Skye Jethani

Made to Flourish
10901 Lowell Avenue
Overland Park, Kansas 66210
madetoflourish.org
communications@madetoflourish.org

Cover design and creative direction: Eric Rivier
Interior design: Eric Rivier and Daniel Carroll

ISBN 9798669202408

Printed in the United States of America
Second Edition

Contents

Preface

Our mission is to empower pastors and their churches to integrate faith, work, and economic wisdom for the flourishing of their communities. To fulfill our mission, we begin by teaching pastors the vital importance of striving for personal wholeness and then providing pastors with rich theological content that underscores the importance of teaching their congregants' faith, work, and economic wisdom (FWE) theology at the foundational level.

Pastors are introducing this rich theology to their churches through four main channels: corporate worship, pastoral practice, discipleship/spiritual formation, and outreach and mission. In fact, this book grew out of conversations we've had with many pastors across the country who have intentionally committed to introducing these ideas and practices in their local churches.

We interviewed 16 pastors for this project; those pastors and churches are listed on the next page.

Below are the pastors and leaders quoted throughout the book.

Stan Archie
Christian Fellowship Baptist Church
Kansas City, Missouri

Ryan Beattie
Bellevue Presbyterian Church
Bellevue, Washington

Brad Beier
Living Hope Church
Chicago, Illinois

Ken Duncan
Jefferson Assembly of God
Meriden, Kansas

Jason Harris
Central Presbyterian Church
New York, New York

Jeremy Lile
City Hope Church
Akron, Ohio

Artie Lindsay
Tabernacle Community Church
Grand Rapids, Michigan

Jim Mullins
Redemption Church
Tempe, Arizona

Tom Nelson
Christ Community Church
Kansas City, Missouri

Mike Reading
United Evangelical Free Church
Seattle, Washington

Gail Roberts-House
Open Door Full Gospel Baptist
Church
Hampton, Virginia

Jay Slocum
Jonah's Call
Pittsburgh, Pennsylvania

Fernando Tamara
Orange County
First Assembly of God
Santa Ana, California

Joe Tucker
South Street Ministries
Associated with Front Porch
Fellowship Church
Akron, Ohio

Jon Tyson
Trinity Grace Church
New York, New York

Larry Ward
Abundant Life Church
Boston, Massachusetts

Foreword

I remember a wise mentor repeatedly reminding me that leaders have to have clarity of purpose and mission. One of his favorite phrases still rings in my ears. "If there is a mist in the pulpit, there will be a fog in the pew." Good advice for sure, but what happens when there is a fog in the pulpit?

A few years into my pastoral ministry, I was forced to confront this compelling question. In spite of my pastoral diligence, packed schedule, and the best of intentions, there was a dense fog in my pulpit. I faced an inconvenient truth. I had been committing pastoral malpractice. I had spent the minority of my time equipping my congregation for what they had been called by God to do the majority of their lives. Rather than narrowing the Sunday to Monday gap that many in my congregation were experiencing, I had actually been helping it widen. My impoverished theological vision was impairing our congregation's spiritual formation, our contribution to the common good, and our local church's gospel mission.

Pastoral repentance was in order. I am most grateful for Christ Community Church, a gracious congregation that was ready to forgive my failings and move forward, guided by a more robust theology of vocation. In *Christian Mission in the Modern World*, John Stott concluded that "We must begin with vocation." But what does this mean? I believe it means that we must see the entire biblical text as a coherent narrative of creation, fall, redemption, and consummation, revealing God's design and desire for human flourishing. I also believe we must regain the transforming truth that the gospel speaks to every aspect of human existence, calling us to discipleship in all areas of life.

Scripture tells us that, as image bearers, we have been created by a working God – with work in mind. That means, in part, that we have been created with community and collaboration in mind; work is not an isolated activity, but an interdependent one. We presently live in a broken and fallen world where our work is not what it ought to be. The good news is that, through the redemptive work of Jesus, the work we do and the workplaces we inhabit are profoundly changed by the gospel.

For those of us who have been called to the pastoral vocation, the implications of a more robust theology of vocation and discipleship reshape not only our thinking, but also our pastoral priorities and practices. Our reading diet will adjust to help us better understand the Monday world of our congregation. A pastoral visit to the workplace of a congregation member will become as common as a visit to the hospital. Our preaching will look and sound different. Our discipleship and spiritual formation pathways will change. With a growing understanding of the church's mission in the world, we will enthusiastically embrace our congregation's everyday work life. We will grasp with new conviction and passion that economic flourishing matters and that a primary work of the church is the church at work. Empowered and guided by the Holy Spirit, the local church we serve will be more faithful to Christ and more effective in furthering the common good.

This is why my heart leaps with joy that you are carving out time to read and reflect on what pastors across the country are doing to help their people connect Sunday to Monday.

I am most grateful for the many opportunities to roll up my sleeves and serve the Made to Flourish pastor's network. I pray that this book will inform your mind, strengthen your pastoral practice, enliven your worship experience, stir your heart, and ultimately shape the congregations and cities you serve. May our churches be all Jesus desires them to be and may we who have been called to the pastoral vocation one day hear: "Well done good and faithful servant, enter into the joy of your Master."

Tom Nelson

Senior Pastor, Christ Community Church

Introduction

"I would love to equip our people to connect their faith with their work, but I don't know where to start."

I was talking with the senior pastor of a large church. The church is by no means perfect, but they are a healthy congregation, with humble leaders who are Christ-centered, Spirit-led, and biblically grounded. They want to answer Jesus' commission to make disciples who follow everything he commanded. And they long for these disciples to follow Jesus in all places, at all times.

But as they sought to live out this worthy desire, they began to realize a blind spot. They hadn't spent much time thinking about where the disciples in their church spent a majority of their time — at work. They certainly hadn't talked about how faith in Jesus applied to concrete work contexts and situations.

Therefore, the congregation was unintentionally formed to think that faith had nothing (or little) to do with everyday work. What does faith in Christ have to do with selling cars?

Or building housing? Or helping people with their financial investments? Or teaching? Or any number of a thousand other careers?

CHANGING CULTURAL CONTEXT

Many pastors and cultural observers have noted that our culture has moved from a Christendom context, where the major power brokers and institutions of our culture cooperated with Christianity or were at least faith-neutral, to a post-Christendom context, where the major power brokers and institutions of our culture do not necessarily cooperate with Christianity or are faith-opposed.

This can be likened to swimming in a river. In Christendom, Christians swim along with the current of the river. Influence is assumed. Shared goals and warm-hearted mutual appreciation is common. In post-Christendom, Christians swim against the current of the river. Everything is harder. The paradigm and posture moves from influence and power over culture, to faithfulness and humility within culture. Christians are exiles living in Babylon, not Jerusalem.

This phenomenon is more or less true depending on the region of the country, but everyone seems to agree that we are all going in this direction, even if some places and cities have been there for a long time. Without being melodramatic, we can say that Christians now swim against the current.

A CHANGED WORK ENVIRONMENT

This has profound implications for workers. It is likely that a majority of our congregation members feel tension about their faith in their place of work.

1. They may be shy about letting others know about their Christian faith.
2. They may be eager to demonstrate they live differently than many of the embarrassing stereotypes people have of Christians and may be tempted to overcorrect.
3. They may never have thought deeply about how Christian theology both affirms and promotes their vocational field, as well as challenges certain elements of their vocational field.
4. They may have few, if any practices, to ground the gospel or the presence of Christ into their hearts amidst their place of work.
5. They may be unsure of how to wrestle with ethical issues brought about by their work.
6. They may feel alone and isolated amidst a work environment with few other Christians.
7. They may have little imagination for the ways faith plays out at work.
8. They may have already decided that both faith and work are important, but like oil and water, they do not mix well.

These challenges (and there are a thousand others), are prime opportunities for the church of Jesus Christ to shepherd people, in what David Kinnaman at Barna has called, "vocational discipleship."

In many ways, this is nothing new. In fact, it is *really* old.

When tax collectors came to be baptized by John the Baptist, they were curious what role faith might have on their lives. John applied faith (repentance) to work. "Don't collect any more than you are required to" (Luke 3:13). For John, the first obligation of faith was an implication for work. John the Baptizer ran a faith and work ministry.

Still, there is a practical question for churches. How then shall we worship? Where do we start? A sermon on faith and work? A prayer for workers on Labor Day Sunday? A small group study on faith and work? Are there other options?

CRAWL, WALK, RUN

A friend at a prominent church articulated how she worked at her church to begin equipping people to integrate faith and work. She decided the church would first need to crawl, then walk, then run. In other words, she wasn't trying to do everything at once. She knew she needed to define some early wins that she could build on.

In your church context you might be new to this endeavor and trying to clarify an easy win around faith and work. Or, you may be down the road a little bit, and it is time to take the next step. Some of you have been a part of this movement for some time and there are further initiatives that will be more appropriate. As you read the book, you might consider what your church's progression through crawl, walk, run, might be.

WHAT THIS BOOK IS NOT

First, this book does not provide theological grounding for

churches to help their people integrate faith with work. That is a worthy project, and one that has been undertaken by many able authors. Relevant books include *Work Matters* (Tom Nelson), *Every Good Endeavor* (Tim Keller), *Why Business Matters to God* (Jeff Van Duzer), and *Whatever You Do: Six Foundations for an Integrated Life* (Luke Bobo, editor). For a pastor or leader wanting to take a first step in learning about faith and work, any of these books would be a great place to start.

Second, this book does not provide biblical exegesis on relevant texts and biblical themes for faith and work. Again, this is a worthy project. We recommend the *Theology of Work Commentary*,[1] which traces the relevant faith and work themes and verses in every book of the Bible.

This book is also not a how-to for individual workers on ways to integrate their faith and their work. Many of the books listed above give handles on what that can look like. This is a growing field with books being written for many different kinds of work and workers.

Lastly, this book is not meant to be a one-size-fits-all approach. We are not advocating a particular study, or a particular curriculum, or a particular method. We believe that 10 different churches might help their congregations integrate faith and work in 10 unique ways.

WHAT THIS BOOK IS

This book is an example manual for pastors and churches interested in exploring tangible steps and practices a church can implement to help equip people integrate faith and work.

It is a birds-eye view of what many different kinds of churches in many different places are doing or have done. We have interviewed pastors and leaders at sixteen churches, gathering data and practical examples that we share in each chapter.

In *Discipleship with Monday in Mind*, we have organized the examples and practices into four categories or themes, which represent different aspects of a healthy church: pastoral practices, the corporate worship gathering, discipleship and spiritual formation, and mission and outreach.

We have done this for several reasons. First, there might be a tendency for churches to create a faith and work ministry as one silo within the church. Integrating faith and work should never be *merely* a silo ministry of the church. The four-fold division we use represents how a church can move beyond a one-off series or a particular program to integrate faith and work.

Second, we believe these four categories can apply to any *size* of church, any *form* of church, and any *ministry* of the church. Most churches, no matter how simple or how complex, no matter how organic or how organized, are active around these four themes, even if the particular language may vary from church to church.

We want to provide frameworks and examples for you to discern the best approach for your church. But you will need to discern what is best given your context.

Finally, the examples we explore in this book are by no means exhaustive. In many ways, this book is still being written, as churches and leaders across the country find new ways to equip the body of Christ for the good works God has planned for them amidst their everyday work. At the writing of this introduction, more than 3,000 pastors have joined the Made to Flourish network. As a network, we regularly hear stories from pastors and leaders that are worthy of being shared but are not yet incorporated into this book.

The goal of all this activity is God's glory. Colossians 3:23 commands (and invites) us, "And whatever you do, in word or deed, do it all in the name of the Lord Jesus, giving thanks to God the Father through him."

We pray that in some way, the content of this book would spur you to equip your congregation to more faithfully do everything, including their everyday work, in the name of the Lord Jesus, to the glory of God. Our great God is worthy of no less.

Matt Rusten

Executive Director, Made to Flourish

Pastoral Practice

Something remarkable happened to ministry in the middle of the 20th century — it moved inside. Perhaps that is over-stating the change. Pastors have served within churches as long as Christians have had purpose-built facilities. What's changed is how much time most pastors spend within those buildings.

Consider what a typical church's ministry looked like a hundred years ago. Each Sunday the community gathered for worship, sacrament, and the preaching of Scripture, and the pastor often organized and led these Sunday gatherings. Like the rest of the congregation, however, the pastor spent most of his time Monday through Saturday outside the church building. He visited his church members in their homes, farms, and factories where he blessed their work and encouraged them to live faithfully with God and one another. He also made calls to the sick and perhaps to those in jail. For most of Christian history ministry happened primarily outside the walls of the church, which is why most church facilities could remain relatively small.

Today, few pastors are trained to carry out their calling in this manner. Instead they are expected to stay inside the church all week, and their activities are usually focused more on operating programs and overseeing a staff than on the daily shepherding of the flock. When the sheep do require pastoral care, counseling, prayer, or instruction, only in rare circumstances — like hospitalization — is the pastor expected to leave his church office. Rather than engaging people where they work, we now expect the people to visit the pastor where he or she works. That represents a dramatic shift in pastoral practice from the previous 19 centuries of Christian ministry.

The point of this history lesson is not to criticize newer modes of ministry or to awaken nostalgia for the past. Each has its own strengths and shortcomings. Instead, we need to recognize how modern pastoral practices may help or hinder the integration of faith, work, and economic wisdom (FWE) within our congregations today. As we interviewed pastors around the country with a commitment to FWE, we found that many engaged in practices uncommon among those trained in contemporary models of ministry. Instead, they were recovering pastoral habits from the past.

In this chapter, we will look at three of the most frequently cited pastoral practices. None of these are difficult to engage, nor do they require elaborate restructuring of a church's programming. These are activities an individual pastor or church leader may begin independently — no new programs to create or budgets to approve. For that reason, these practices may be the best place for a pastor seeking to integrate faith, work, and economic wisdom into their congregation to begin.

PASTORAL PRACTICE ONE: CURIOSITY

The first practice is more accurately identified as a proclivity. It's an attitude or disposition that the other practices are predicated upon. Although rarely identified as a pastoral characteristic, curiosity is an essential quality of any person called to shepherd and equip God's people.

One of the most frequent metaphors for leadership in Scripture is shepherding. David identified the Lord as his shepherd in the Old Testament, and Jesus referred to himself as the Good Shepherd in the New Testament. That is why throughout the Bible the leaders of God's people are also identified as "shepherds" (see Jeremiah 23 and 1 Peter 5). They are called to represent the character of God to his people. Even the title pastor means "shepherd."

What makes this metaphor so compelling is the trust and intimacy that must exist between shepherds and sheep. The shepherd leads, feeds, and protects the flock. As Jesus said, "The sheep follow him, because they know his voice ... I am the good shepherd. I know my own, and my own know me" (John 10:4, 15). It is a profoundly relational image of pastoral leadership.

To shepherd well, pastors must know their sheep. This was a trait we observed consistently among the church leaders we interviewed. They were incredibly curious about the people God had entrusted to their care. These pastors studied their congregations, they sought to understand their lives and contexts, and they gave particular attention to the vocations of their people. They wanted to know what their sheep did Monday through Saturday and how they did it. They were inquisitive leaders.

For example, when Jon Tyson, of Trinity Grace Church, first arrived in New York City to plant a church, he recognized that he could not effectively pastor his growing congregation without investigating their vocations. "I started subscribing to a bunch of emails about current events in various industries that particularly affected the people in my congregation," he reported. He still dedicates time every week to reading books about these industries. His goal is not to become an expert, but to be familiar enough to have meaningful conversations with people about their work.

Tyson says his commitment to studying the vocations of his church members and neighbors is often met with surprise. "I'll meet someone in a coffee shop or one of my neighbors and ask them what they do. When I share something I know about their work they'll say, 'Oh my gosh, you're a pastor? I can't believe you know about that.' It happens all the time."

Tyson is clear, however: "The goal is not to impress them but to connect with them." His curiosity continues to drive the conversation. "I tell the person that I actually don't know that much about their work," he said, "And I ask them, 'Please tell me more.' That puts me in the posture of being the learner and the other person in the position of the expert."

Like Tyson, other pastors reported that reading broadly in the industries represented in their congregations was very important, as well as not limiting one's studying to ministry principles or church management. "The problem with so many ministry books," one pastor told me, "is that they assume every church's context is the same. They offer plug-and-play solutions that may work in one place but not in another."

I (Skye) discovered this reality in 2008 not long after the full effects of the Great Recession were being felt. I was asked to speak at a church and consult with its leadership team. They were interested in learning how to attract more young adults to their church. After a few days, however, I discovered through thoughtful conversations with church members that a significant number of them worked in construction and real estate — two industries that were disproportionately impacted by the recession. I also learned that the CEO of one of the largest employers connected to the church had just committed suicide.

These facts drastically changed how I coached the church's pastoral team. "Your congregation is hurting right now," I told them. "They're scared about their jobs and worried about the future.

This isn't the time to launch a new program to reach young adults." Although they had the best of intentions, the pastors' focus on reaching young adults had come from attending ministry conferences and reading popular ministry books. Put bluntly, they were more curious about what was happening in other large churches than what was happening in their immediate community. They didn't know their sheep.

Don't assume that practicing curiosity means immediately reallocating hours of your time to reading about agriculture or financial derivatives. It can be as simple as asking good questions. Kent Duncan of Jefferson Assembly of God, for example, says that when he meets with members of his church, he is much more intentional about asking about their vocation. It isn't a perfunctory question like, "How's work?" Instead, Duncan inquires more meaningfully. "Can you tell me about your work?" is a better question. He wants to understand the significance of what they do throughout the week.

This essential quality of pastoral curiosity grows when we begin to put the life and context of our sheep ahead of our agenda as shepherds — when we recognize that genuinely seeking to understand their callings is part of our calling.

PASTORAL PRACTICE TWO: WORKPLACE VISITATIONS

Once a shepherd begins to cultivate a growing curiosity about the lives of the sheep, it will inevitably lead him or her out into the pastures where the sheep spend the majority of their time. In other words, curiosity pushes pastors outside the church walls and into the work environments of church members. Regularly visiting people at their work was by far the most cited, and most transformative, pastoral practice we uncovered in our interviews.

Most people are surprised when a pastor asks to visit their work. Pastor Mike Reading of United Evangelical Free Church said he's been talking about faith and work from the pulpit for some time, but members of his church were still unsure what to think about his interest in seeing where they work. "I find that they're mostly like, 'All right, but what are you going to do if you come to my office?' They're concerned about how I will carry myself, but for the most part they are really flattered."

Reading says workplace visitations are essential for him to understand people's lives. "I go to where people work, eat lunch with them, try to see their office, try to know what they experience, because it fascinates me." These visitations function as reconnaissance missions for pastors like Reading. They provide a fuller picture of what the congregation's needs and opportunities really are. This information is valuable when planning sermons or church initiatives.

It also provides deeper insight into people's gifts and abilities. Reading shared about one church member he described as a "stoic intellectual."

> This guy didn't show much emotion at all in church, but when I went to his office, he was like a kid. I never got to see that part of him before, but it came out when he worked.

Mike sees the time he spends in church members' offices as "fruitful and helpful to the church." It's also a way of making members "feel more affirmed and supported by the church." In other words, workplace visitation is a practice that simultaneously informs the pastor as it affirms the member.

Stan Archie of Christian Fellowship Baptist Church likes to take things a step beyond mere visitations. He asks church members if he can do "ride alongs" where he'll spend half a day shadowing them at their work. Archie reported:

> We had a guy who was a homebuilder at our church. I used to go to the sites with him and do

the inspections together. That gave me a real
feel for what his life was like, and it allowed me
to make sure the church was offering legit-
imate, practical, biblical foundations for the
reality of his daily living.

Some pastors might be uncomfortable asking a church
member for a ride along, but starting to practice workplace
visitations doesn't have to be difficult. Once again, it all starts
with curiosity. Kent Duncan had a conversation with a church
member who managed a printing operation. After a few questions about his work, Duncan learned they just purchased
a new printing machine. "I'd like to come see that," he told
the member. Now he's making plans to visit his congregant's
workplace and start connecting with him there.

Obviously, some workplaces are easier to visit than others.
Duncan reported, "With some blue-collar workers you can't
always see them on the plant floor, but they're absolutely
happy to talk about their work." When a pastor shows that he
cares for them, prays about their work, and makes an effort
to affirm it, "It is a very positive experience."

Other pastors shared creative ways to get outside the church
building and into the workplace environments of their people.
Meetings, as we all know, are a necessary part of every ministry.
Larry Ward of Abundant Life Church tries whenever possible to
hold a meeting at the member's place of business rather than
at the church. "I say, 'Do you mind if I come to your office?'
That way I don't simply allow them to come to the church."

Jim Mullins and John Crawford of Redemption Church have

even taken many pastors' most isolating task, sermon prep, and moved it outside the church. Mullins reports:

> A lot of our pastors prepare their sermons in the places where people live and move and have their being. Last week I prepared my sermon in a hospital cafeteria. Sometimes we'll go to industrial areas or onto the campus of Arizona State University. We want the places where our people live and work to shape the sermons we preach to them.

The interviews we conducted taught us that church leaders need to seek opportunities to get outside the church and into the workplaces of their people. Conduct one-on-one meetings, or even church committee meetings, in someone else's workplace. Meet church members at their office for lunch. Inquire about their jobs and ask to learn more by visiting the site. You may even find people willing to let you shadow them for part of the day. The information you gather and the affirmation you show is likely to transform both you and your church.

PASTORAL PRACTICE THREE: PRAYER AND COUNSELING
Having a fuller understanding of church members' vocations and workplaces also shifts the way pastors pray for their people. This becomes visible not only in the corporate worship gatherings, but also in the weekly practices of the pastor between Sundays.

After Larry Ward started incorporating workplace visitations into his pastoral routine, he found more members were inviting him to their offices. A schoolteacher came to Ward and said, "Pastor, would you come to my classroom and pray?" The public school, for obvious reasons, wouldn't allow prayer in the classroom with the students, but Ward came in just before the students arrived and prayed with the teacher, "and the school allowed us to do it." His presence and prayer helped the teacher view her work and classroom as a sacred calling and space. It shifted her vision of her work.

Another member of Ward's church oversees a laboratory that conducts tests on cells. He invited Ward to the lab to "pray over us as we do our testing." By getting out of the church and into the laboratory, Ward is affirming the value of these scientists' work and asking for the Lord's presence to empower their research.

Jon Tyson said that when he visits a workplace, he often asks the church member how they hope to see God's kingdom in their work. That often leads to prayer not just for the church member, but for the business and everyone who works there. Tyson told us of one ministry opportunity that has resulted from this practice:

> We had a guy at our church with some influence within a startup business. It has now done really well. Sometimes he will reserve a conference room when I meet him there. The two of us will spend an hour praying together for the kingdom of God to come into that company, for the encouragement of its leaders, and for people's salvation.

To those who pass by it may look like Tyson is being interviewed for a job, but it is actually ministry that is happening.

Prayer is a significant way pastors care for their people, and so is counseling. Some of the church leaders we interviewed reported a shift in their counseling practices as well. "I view vocational counseling as just as important as marriage counseling," said Jim Mullins. "Both marriage and work are found in Genesis 1 and 2, but the church only tends to put effort into helping marriages. I think that [marriage] is really important, but so is our work in the world."

Of course, in some cases being curious about church members' work may uncover serious problems requiring pastoral intervention. Jon Tyson, for example, said it is common in a place like Manhattan to discover a church member has made an idol of their work. Mike Reading shared the story of visiting a church member at his office and discovering his work was all-consuming. Reading recalled,

> It prompted a great conversation about his tendency to give his best energy to his work and have nothing left for his family. Now I'm focusing on how to help his marriage. I don't think he would have been that vulnerable with me if he hadn't first felt affirmed by me in his work.

We have found that pastors who effectively integrate faith, work, and economic wisdom into their congregations engage in practices that take them outside the church and into the workplaces of their people. This changes how they pray, how they counsel, and even how they preach. It all begins, however, with curiosity — a genuine desire to understand the people entrusted to their care and the work God has called them to. The weekly routines of ministry change when shepherds make it a priority to know their sheep.

Corporate Worship

The language we use when we gather as a church community is not neutral. If we are not careful our language can inadvertently perpetuate the unbiblical idea that there is a delineation between sacred and secular work. Language used in worship can also unintentionally elevate white-collar work while denigrating blue-collar work.

Artie Lindsay, pastor of Tabernacle Community Church, knows this tendency well and takes pains to avoid it. "We are very careful with our language," he says. Lindsay and others are careful not to use "secular/sacred" kind of talk or "full-time ministry" language. And all members at Tabernacle are constantly reminded, "You're valued and loved by God." They attempt to help their congregants see that *everyone* is in full-time ministry. Of course, this emphasis dovetails well with biblical teaching of the "priesthood of all believers" (1 Peter 2:4-10).

When we asked Lindsay to share a story of a church member who has imbibed this theology of faith and work integration, he recounted the story of Vickie.

One of Lindsay's congregants, Vickie, has taken his teaching on the impor- tance of faith-and-work integration to heart and it has influenced her work. Initially, however, Vickie, a Christian, was not even a believer in this faith-and-work integration idea. In fact, she was quite cynical, not believing God cared for her work in

emergency rooms, taking people's insurance. When Lindsay began talking to Vickie about her work, Vickie was less than receptive. "Pastor Artie keeps talking about this, but doesn't know what I do. I am a paper pusher." However, as she continued to meet with Lindsay and listen to him, her heart softened. Eventually, she became a believer. Today she sees what she does in light of her faith. "God was using me to bring care to people during one of their most difficult and stressful of situations."

Pastor Tom Nelson of Christ Community Church adds:

> We have deliberately abandoned language that perpetuates the dualism of the world to elevate the spiritual world over the material world; we have jettisoned language that devalues the temporal in light of the eternal; we have 'retired' language that elevates certain vocations over others and language that diminishes the fullness of God's redemptive program and the goodness of all creation.

Nelson and his staff avoid phrases such as "secular work," "kingdom work," "full-time Christian work," and "moving from success to significance." They're similarly careful to avoid language that minimizes temporality. They avoid ideas encapsulated in expressions like "living for the line (eternity) rather than the dot (temporality)." They also try to eschew devaluing the material world with phrases like, "It is all going to burn," or "What really matters are people's souls." Another common phrase they've jettisoned is, "Make your life count for God," since it can diminish people's sense of their intrinsic value as embodied image bearers in the here and now.

Pastor Fernando Tamara, who formerly worked as an assistant manager at an Italian restaurant, using modified language during the offering period based on Jesus' commandment to love our neighbor as ourselves. He no longer announces the giving period as an opportunity to give "tithes and offerings." Instead, Tamara has chosen to say, "We have a moral obligation to our neighbor." Tamara made this switch because he wants to take the focus off of making money for oneself to making money to benefit one's neighbor. This has taken some time for this idea to take root because many Hispanics come to America for the promise of achieving the American Dream.

Pastor Ryan Beattie of Bellevue Presbyterian Church intentionally invites worshipers to dwell on what happened during the week. Rather than asking they "forget about their cares and concentrate on God" in the corporate worship setting, Beattie asks, "What's on your calendar this week? We're going to sing songs that ask God for wisdom and courage and help [for your work week]. Don't leave [your work concerns] at the door." Beattie stresses the importance of infusing the church context with language around faith and work and the value of work before launching too many programs.

Some churches have gone a step further by incorporating faith and work language into their self-descriptions. At Abundant Life Church, Ward mentioned they are governed by the motto: "A church where faith and life connect." Such language enforces the belief that faith should inform all of life, of which work is a significant part. Reading's church, United Evangelical Free Church, has a motto for his church that is similarly holistic: "Quit trying to be the best church in the city that competes with other churches, and be the best church for the city. Seek to be the kind of church that, if we were to shut our doors, the city would mourn."

At Jonah's Call, Jay Slocum and his pastoral staff have adapted a famous quote from the Dutch theologian Abraham

Kuyper and made it their motto: "There's not a square inch that doesn't belong to Jesus." In fact, faith, work, and economic wisdom (FWE) is written into their church business plan! This has spilled over into the adoption of new language elsewhere in the life of the church. For instance, the director of music isn't called the "worship leader." Why not? Jay explains:

> We don't want our people to think that worship is something that takes place merely on Sunday. It's something we do when we gather, and it's something we do when we scatter.

In other words, work is a form of worship that, when done well and ethically, is done "heartily as unto the Lord" (Col 3:23-25). The language pastors use can perpetuate the secular/spiritual dualism leading to a bifurcated life for congregants. Or a pastor's language can affirm all vocations as good and noble and promote the idea that our work provides a laboratory for growing into christlikeness. As one pastor put it, "Our pastoral language must stimulate and support whole-life discipleship."[2]

AFFIRMING ALL VOCATIONS

All work matters to God. Collecting trash matters to God. Preparing lattes matters to God. Changing dirty diapers matters to God. Cooking a meal matters to God. Developing an Excel spreadsheet matters to God. As someone once said, "If it is not sinful work, it is sacred work." Work is not only sacred but an opportunity to worship. Freddy Williams and David Comstock eloquently explain, "The ability to work is a gift and a sacred practice. Work is an opportunity to worship."[3]

Pastor Gail Roberts-House, a former elementary school principal, loves surprising her congregation. Every quarter, Roberts-House, pastor of Open Door Full Gospel Baptist Church recognizes the work of someone in her congregation. On one occasion, she recognized Larry, a custodian at Hampton University. Larry is an usher and was standing by the door when he heard his name announced on Sunday morning. Roberts-House reported that Larry cried as she presented him with a certificate and pen set. When I asked her how she selects people to recognize, she responded, "I try to select people who are behind the scenes and who are unassuming."

To communicate the sacredness of work, many churches have "Faith at Work" interviews during the worship service. For example, every six weeks, pastor Brad Beier at Living Hope Church, interviews a church member.

During the interview, Beier asks five basic questions:

1. What type of work do you do?
2. How do you try to do that work as a Christian?
3. How does sin seem to affect that work?
4. How do you try to serve your neighbors through your work?
5. How can we pray for you?

Not only does Beier conduct "Faith at Work" interviews, he has also incorporated a version of this in their children's ministry. They take what they do upfront for the congregation and "reduce it into a more bite-sized package" for children. Child-friendly props are brought in, and teachers ask questions like "What do you want to do when you grow up?" and "How can you serve Jesus through that type of work?" The aim is to get children thinking about faith and work at an early age.

Pastor Mike Reading takes a different approach. They emphasize, celebrate, and affirm a different industry each month. In January 2016, it was education. In February it was finance. And recently it was celebrating those in the technology industry. Reading chooses a person in that industry to interview and he asks these basic questions:

1. What do you do?
2. How did you feel called to do what you're doing?
3. What are certain opportunities or obstacles you're facing in your work?
4. How does your faith speak to those obstacles?
5. How can we pray for you?

At the conclusion of the interview, Reading invites all congregants in that particular industry to stand and he leads a commissioning service much like they would to commission a missionary going abroad.

Many churches do variations of what Reading and Beier do. For instance, Artie Lindsay conducts "all of life" interviews once a month. They have interviewed healthcare professionals, business owners, stay-at-home moms, and students. After the interview, church leaders invite all people in that particular field to stand and the congregation prays for them together.

City Hope Church pastor Jeremy Lile, who refers to himself as a "recovering dualist," dubs these interviews as "stories of servants and stewards," based on 1 Corinthians 4:1. His questions include:

1. How do you co-create with God through the work that you do?
2. Where do you experience the fall and brokenness?
3. Where do you experience restoration and redemption through the work you do?
4. How do you sense that your work is part of God's greater work?

Mullins, who has been doing such interviews over the past two years, believes there is a positive, cumulative effect. In particular, he has noticed that people have a sense of how God made them, and therefore of the good works that they are created to walk in (Eph 2:10). People in their work context understand the stewardship mandate of Genesis 1 and 2, what they are stewarding, and what aspects of God's character are being reflected. And people have taken the command to "love your neighbor as yourself" seriously. And they see their work as a way of loving their neighbor.

One unexpected result has been that local businesses have approached Mullins and his pastoral staff at Redemption Church wanting to hire people from their church. And this includes businesses owned and operated by non-believers! One restaurant, which is known as one of the nicest restaurants in Tempe, Arizona, has even asked Redemption Church staff to lead a retreat for their staff.

MORE ON COMMISSIONING SERVICES

It is a common practice for churches to commission Christians who embark on doing missionary work abroad. Many churches see their congregants entering the workplace — a mission field — on a weekly basis. So, bi-monthly, pastor Jason Harris at Central Presbyterian Church, commissions people to specific vocations in the same way they would pray for pastors or foreign missionaries. They have commissioned those in finance, law, the arts, and the health industry so far. Harris explains that failure to do this "deepens the divide between the sacred and the secular."

Initially, people were not sure why Harris was praying for lawyers. When Harris told a few of the lawyers he would pray for them during the service, some were concerned they would have to bear the brunt of a bad lawyer joke. However, it proved to be a moving and ennobling experience for both the congregation and the lawyers to see them lift up the important work that lawyers do. By commissioning lawyers, Harris and others affirmed that these dear brothers and sisters took their vocation as advocates for their clients seriously.

Similarly, Ryan Beattie has planned and participated in four commissionings for those in many industries. Beattie, whose church is located in the shadow of Microsoft and Amazon, has commissioned workers in such industries as technology and computer and software engineering. He has also commissioned his congregants who labor in the fields of marketing, medicine, and finance.

Beattie explained how when they first began, they had to coax people to stand up, and they had to explain to the congregation what they were doing and why they were doing it. After commissioning those in the tech industry one Sunday morning, a female visitor hurriedly approached Beattie and said, "It's our first Sunday visiting here. My husband had never seen his faith relating to his work." The commissioning service was powerful for this man. Such examples simply underscore the fact that we were never meant to live a compartmentalized life; our faith should inform our parenting, our citizenship, and our work.

Pastor Jon Tyson, who providentially bumped into Steve Garber in Washington, D.C., recounted a conversation they had. Garber told Tyson that he had heard about his work in New York and kindly offered him this suggestion:

> There are people who labor all week long and you bring missionaries up front and you pray for them, and you commission and send them out. Wouldn't it be an amazing thing if you could take the people and send them into the city that you love so much, so that they felt like missionaries to their industries?

Tyson recalled that the conversation with Garber had a "liturgical shaping force." Since that crucial conversation with Garber, Tyson has employed a new practice before preaching. Before opening the Word, he invites a person representing a particular vocation to come forward. For example, he might have a schoolteacher come up and read a prayer for all educators. Then all teachers are invited to stand and the congregation claps and cheers for them as they are commissioned in their vocation.

Such commissioning services can have a similar "liturgical shaping" impact on others. For example, after doing a commissioning service, a teacher approached Tyson and said, "That was the most powerful moment in *my entire life* in church. Thank you." Commissioning services have a powerful ability to affirm people in their work.

TRADITIONAL AND NONTRADITIONAL SERMONS

The sermon in a worship service provides an ideal time to teach on the importance of faith and work integration. Larry Ward preaches a sermon series around Labor Day weekend with a prayer and commissioning service. One benefit of such preaching and teaching is that Abundant Life Church is attracting and retaining millennials.

Ward told us that the millennials he ministers to don't like talking about "careers" as much as "callings." They want to believe their work is more than a job for personal advancement. They want to understand how their work relates to a larger vision — how it contributes to the common good and even to God's cosmic purposes. So, teaching on faith and work is helping millennials to make a concrete connection on how they can use their knowledge, gifts, and talents to make a difference in the lives of others.

Sometimes in place of traditional sermons, Ward hosts "forums." These forums feature people from different occupations who talk about what they do and why it's beneficial for people. So far, Ward has had a funeral director, an insurance agent, and a human resources professional participate in these forums. After the presentation, congregants are encouraged to ask questions of the presenters. Often there are more questions than there is time to answer them. Ward doesn't mind substituting a forum for a traditional sermon because he wants his people to view work as part of the "all of life" discipleship process.

Roberts-House, also in place of a traditional sermon, will serve as the moderator of a panel. On one particular Sunday, the panelists included a sergeant major, school bus driver, manager of a local restaurant, nurse practitioner, and a special education teacher. With their photos projected on the sanctuary big screen, Roberts-House asked the panelists such questions as, "How do you integrate your faith and your work?" and "How has your faith created a different work atmosphere?"

Kent Duncan, who did his D.Min. on introducing the theology and practice of faith, work, and economics to his mostly blue-collar congregation, developed a four-week study where each Sunday was devoted to a faith-work topic. Duncan noted that his context is particularly difficult because there is often animosity between upper management and those on the assembly line. Animosity is often exacerbated when management exhibits an attitude that says, "You do the work, we'll do the thinking. And by the way, we need more production out of you." That communicates to a blue-collar worker that their work does not matter. At the end of his sermon series, Duncan did a commissioning service for these blue-collar workers. These workers were brought to the front of the sanctuary and his elders came and laid hands on them. Then the entire congregation prayed that God would make these brothers and sisters flourish in their callings.

At the end of the prayer, one female member said, "That was the most significant prayer anybody ever prayed for me." Duncan found that his congregation was "wonderfully receptive to the whole series on work because he was finally talking about something that mattered to them." Work matters to God — and it matters to congregants, too.

Because the preaching moment is such an excellent opportunity to teach, Jason Harris of Central Presbyterian Church tries to incorporate anecdotes and illustrations that draw from the variety of vocations represented by his members. Doing so, he said, speaks of those vocations in a way that affirms the dignity of the vocation. "There's a lot of people who may be in a particular profession, and when they hear the profession mentioned in the sermon, it's done in a very derogatory way." For example, businesspeople are often assumed to be greedy and politicians are assumed to be dishonest or self-serving. But by using stories drawn from the workplace that cast congregants' professions in a positive light, Harris is able to counter those negative perceptions and affirm their callings.

Discipleship and Spiritual Formation

In Lester DeKoster's *Work: The Meaning of Your Life*, he explains that our work is forming the world, and our work is forming us. On one hand, we are forming the world through the agency of our work, and on the other hand, our work provides a laboratory for growing in christlikeness. In light of this dual purpose, we must integrate our faith and our work through intentional discipleship. Churches are seeking this intentional discipleship in diverse ways.

STARTING WITH THE BASICS

In their discipleship setting, Reading starts with the basics.

> I spend a lot of time connecting people to God's intent for creation, God's desire for industries, and the renewal of all things. The ships of Tarshish, the industries — they're still going to be in the New Heavens and New Earth. The culture

of cities and nations will still be there. It will be purified in glorifying God. I sense the biggest need is for my people to have a positive view of our city and culture. And it's been a very slow process to communicate that, especially with a city like Seattle that can be so anti-Christian.

Pastor Jeremy Lile is currently going through a book with a group of men. In these groups a space has been created where all are invited to talk openly about the successes and struggles that they are experiencing at work. Lile has also taken his larger community through the *FLOW*[4] series. He was delighted that this series led to robust conversations about God, work, and vocation. Likewise, pastor Beier has hosted "Table Talk Discussions," an onsite Bible study for after Sunday worship. On a quarterly basis, Beier takes four to six weeks to focus on a discipleship topic with a group over lunch. Beier also used *FLOW* — with some adaptation — because in his urban context many come from severely broken homes and many of the *FLOW* episodes present an idyllic picture of the family.

Artie Lindsay creatively convened what Tabernacle Community Church calls *LIVE* Team (Leadership in Vocational Engagement). Here, a group of 12 people read and worked through Amy Sherman's book, *Kingdom Calling*. The hope is that this core group will develop a robust view of the kingdom that will be infused into the life of the church, and ultimately will impact the city as well. Tabernacle does not have an adult Sunday School. However, Lindsay wants to develop a faith, work, and economics curriculum for middle school students to introduce them to a theology of work.

IN-HOUSE CURRICULUM DEVELOPMENT

Christ Community Church, under the leadership of Tom Nelson, has developed its own curriculum designed to provide guidance from "cradle to grave." The church's children's ministry has icons and banners prominently displayed with these words: *Ought* (Creation), *Is* (Fall), *Can* (Redemption), and *Will* (Restoration/Consummation). Nelson explains that the four-chapter story is embedded into the discipleship DNA of Christ Community Church.

Mullins and other staff at Redemption Church have also created their own curriculum in-house. However, he admits that this development generally involves synthesizing a number of off-the-shelf materials.

Pastor Duncan's teaching and preaching was reinforced through concurrent small group Bible studies that explored his sermon topics more deeply. One topic they explored that is often overlooked in the FWE conversation is the significance of the Sabbath. Duncan's teaching sessions communicated the significance of this topic to his members. The small group Bible study material was developed using materials such as "Work is Worship"[5] and adapted Acton Institute materials on economic and human flourishing.

When Duncan was asked for an example of a church member who has imbibed this theology of faith and work integration and is now living it out, he proudly spoke of Mike.

As you may remember, Duncan ministers to a congregation composed mostly of blue-collar workers. The importance of faith and work integration has been a hard sell for his congregation. However, Duncan relayed the story of Mike, a young man who worked at a local print shop cutting dog food labels. After listening to Duncan's sermon series on faith and work, and after going through the small group Bible study, Mike was able to make a connection between Adam's creative activity in the garden in cooperation with God and his job of cutting dog food labels. He proudly said, "Even if I'm cutting dog food labels, I'm making something that wasn't there before. I'm cooperating with God in the creation of something new." This sharp young man appreciated the connection between his ordinary labor and what God wanted through his work at that time in his life.

SEMINARS

Instead of a traditional adult Sunday School, Central Presbyterian Church hosts a seminar series called Vocare. Pastor Harris described the purpose of this seminar as a tool "To explore the intersection between the gospel culture and vocation, thinking through how we live out our call as God's people in the world in light of the challenges and opportunities of our cultural moment." Speakers have included those from academia, including David Miller, director of the Princeton University Faith and Work Initiative, and Steve Garber, professor of marketplace theology and leadership at Regent College (Vancouver, Canada), and director of Regent's new graduate program, the Master of Arts in Leadership, Theology, and Society.

When Harris was asked to share the story of a church member who has connected a theology of faith and work and is now living it out, he recounted the following story about a CEO from his congregation. Prior to moving to New York and attending our church, this CEO was living in another city functioning as the head of a different company. They had purchased another company, and the acquisition required an enormous amount of time and energy on his part. It was a great success, and he was excited about being part of this accomplishment. But he told me that that following Sunday, as he sat in church, he had this sad moment where he realized that nothing that was happening at church spoke to what he'd been working on. No one knew. And even if they did know, it wouldn't have really mattered to them. I think for him this experience of sadness arose out of how deep this divide can be between the church and the workplace. So, he, on more than one occasion, has told me just how much he has personally enjoyed and benefited from this seminar series.

SHAPING CHILDREN, YOUTH, AND FAMILIES

Mullins admitted that there was a season where Redemption was focusing on people whose jobs already had honor and prestige in society (e.g., doctors, lawyers). They were also focusing exclusively on adults. So, they started something called the "All of Life" camp. The name of the camp is drawn from the tagline of their church, "All of life is all for Jesus." The church takes children who attend the camp to various workplaces where adults are working, and they talk about their work. The goal is to give these students a rich experience within that particular work context. To reinforce what children are hearing on a typical Sunday morning and during the All of Life camps, parents are provided with materials so that they can discuss and reinforce the teachings with their children in the home (see Deut 6:4-9).

VOCATIONAL AFFINITY GROUPS

Some churches have started vocational affinity groups. The idea is to place Christians who serve in the same industry in a small group for mutual encouragement and instruction. Sustaining such groups can be challenging, but under the right conditions, these groups can be quite helpful.

Through their "Vocation Collectives," Mullins attempts to bring people from the same industry together one or two times a year. Here Mullins and other Redemption Church staff help these small groups facilitate a theological reflection on their work. These groups are also encouraged to meet and to pray for each other through the issues that come up in their

work. For Redemption, the key to the sustainability of their vocational affinity groups is their infrequency. Group members are busy, which makes meeting weekly or even monthly unrealistic. But occasional "Vocation Collectives" meetings still foster relational connections that can be sustained outside of official meetings. These deep relational connections outlive the actual small groups. Nelson says that such vocational affinity groups have a relatively short shelf life unless "the relationships deepen into long-term valuable friendships."

Both Nelson and Mullins agree that sustained personal relationships should be the goal rather than sustained vocational groups. Jay Slocum has found that encouraging people to meet up during the natural rhythm of their workday — for example, at lunchtime or in the early morning before the workday begins — aids sustainability. Slocum explains:

> We've empowered them to do really well in their vocations. They're working 50 or 60 hours a week and they're really 'killing it' in the marketplace. [As a consequence] they don't have a huge amount of bandwidth to be a good father or husband if they're taking one night during the week to do something away from their families.

Mullins recounted the story of Mike and Jennifer.

Mike and Jennifer were passionate about work and their faith but didn't know how to combine the two. "You have your spiritual life and you have your occupational life and hobbies you enjoy," Mike and Jennifer said. "We didn't see how the two connected." They felt guilty, wondering if they enjoyed their occupations and hobbies too much. But when Mike and Jennifer caught a vision of how occupational endeavors — in their case, careers in the meat business — could fit into God's economy, and how they can serve and love their neighbors through them, they were enlivened.

HIND-QUARTER.		FORE-QUARTER.	
1.	Sirloin.	10.	Fore rib (5 ribs).
2.	Rump.	11.	Middle rib (4 ribs).
3.	Aitchbone.	12.	Chuck rib (3 ribs).
4.	Buttock.	13.	Leg of mutton piece.
5.	Mouse-round.	14.	Brisket
6.	Veiny piece.	15.	Clod.
7.	Thick flank.	16.	Neck.
8.	Thin flank.	17.	Shank.
9.	Leg.	18.	Cheek.

Eventually their newfound theology of work and faith drove them into getting the training required to become ranchers. It was a three-year process of learning how to run their business in a sustainable way that makes the best, healthiest meat. But they now run a ranch, and they have a theology of ranching! Namely, Mike and Jennifer are applying biblical principles to their entrusted gift: their ranch.

Eight years ago, Tyson launched industry roundtables, which were organized around vocations. These "missional communities" went "very, very well," Tyson reported, and they resonated with people in the community. These were mid-size communities, organized around a particular industry. The purpose of the groups was to explore "theology, ethics, best practices, tensions, and networking." Tyson found that these groups fueled an appetite for further engagement. "Faith and work is like an itch that, once you start scratching it, you can't stop scratching it."

Harris has started putting people together who are in the same industry — and stepping back to see what happens. Recently, a group of CEOs of smaller companies gathered to learn from each other. Prior to this gathering, these CEOs operated in their silos. Harris said the CEOs were grateful to connect with others who understood their challenges. "It's stressful being an entrepreneur and there are not a lot of people these CEOs can talk to about the kind of questions or problems they face."

INTENSIVE DISCIPLESHIP SCHOOLS

Some churches have opted to send their members to formal discipleship schools like Gotham Fellows School,[6] Denver Institute's 5280 Fellowship Program,[7] and Surge.[8]

When we asked a Gotham staff person to share a story of a church member who has lived this out, he recounted the story of a woman who started her own design studio. She became a Christian later in life, then came to Redeemer and went through the Gotham program. She saw her faith as being about serving to meet needs. In her case, that meant doing pro bono design work for nonprofits. What she didn't grasp was the way the gospel transforms everything she did in her workplace, not just how she could serve people in need. She began to look within her own organization to see what practices she and other senior staff were doing with their employees that really acknowledged their humanity and looked to

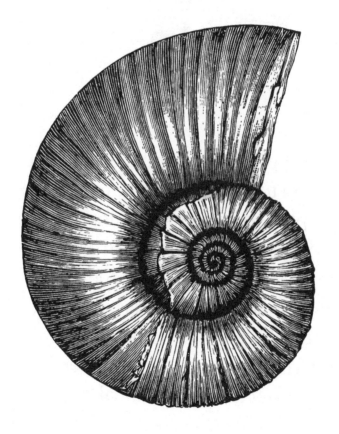

develop them as human beings. She began to explore how she could give employees opportunities for creative expression. She also began examining the work she did and the clients she would take. She was beginning and willing to take some pretty unorthodox kinds of clients because she wanted to be missional, and that meant going to areas that a lot of Christians wouldn't want to go.

There was one client in Colorado who sold marijuana chocolate. She came to me, and we had a long discussion about whether this was something she should take on or not. I gave her enough theological background to wrestle through the question. For instance, in Scripture, God calls his people to be light in some pretty dark places. I wondered aloud whether God might be calling her into this area so that, through her relationships and the way she approaches her work, she might be a loving influence there. Ironically, as a result of going through a church program, she was more open to these clients than if she hadn't gone through it.

Pastor Mullins of Redemption Church is an enthusiastic advocate of Surge. Surge is a 12-month discipleship school that begins with a re-telling of the four chapters of the gospel story: creation, fall, redemption, and restoration. It is during the retelling of the whole gospel story that the instructors also address other topics such as idolatry and sanctification. After laying this theological foundation, the program emphasizes holistic mission. The last session focuses on work and vocation. Just from the Tempe, Arizona area alone, 250 people have matriculated through this intensive discipleship program. Mullins beamed as he recalled the program's impact: "The cumulative effect of having a new class go through it year after year and interact with each other is that this is really shaping culture."

Mission and Outreach

At Made to Flourish, we speak about faith, work, and economic wisdom (FWE). Outreach and missions provide many opportunities to address the "E" in that acronym. We define economics as "the moral and social system of value exchange." Many churches interviewed have ventured into this area to help "the other." However, the approaches to missions and outreach vary widely in terms of how they play out.

Jay Slocum of Jonah's Call has a unique approach to outreach and missions. Jonah's Call does not have an outreach and missions budget, per se. When people ask Slocum, "Why don't you give more to outreach?" he responds, "We give all of our budget to outreach." What does he mean by this? If their people aren't making the city flourish through their work, then they're failing. Slocum explains:

> We may not be getting a lot of credit because
> we run a food bank, but we have people posi-
> tioned in their careers as architects or teachers

or lawyers or legislators or stay-at-home moms who are doing important work.

Slocum is trying to get parishioners to realize that, in the words of Lester DeKoster, some of our work is forming the world, and some of our work is forming us.[9] In other words, our work does double duty. It forms us into being more Christlike and we form our world through the agency of our work. It is the latter that Slocum is equipping his congregants to do.

LIKE-MINDED PARTNERS

Jeremy Lile's church, City Hope, is a startup. In order to maximize their resources, they have pursued partners who are committed to like-minded efforts, like dignity-affirming work. Drawing from the ideas of John Perkins of the Christian Community Development Association (CCDA) that "dignity isn't something that you give someone or take away from them," one of the couples at City Hope described a passion to "feed the hungry and to make food security a reality in the city." All of this led to the starting of "an open-choice food pantry." As the description implies, people have a choice in the groceries that they select at the food pantry.

It's almost like assisted grocery shopping. Plus, the shoppers and those who help them share a meal together! This table meal creates a sense of community, and people now show up and say, "I don't even want groceries this week; I just want to be together as a community." This has taken time because most helpers only see their role as benefactors; people who give things away. Now they are seeing the usefulness of sitting at a table with people and getting to know their story and relating to them.

Lile spoke affectionately of a regular shopper who had been looking for work. When Lile saw him, he asked him how his job search was going. The man replied:

> I just got a temp job, but I think it could develop into something long-term. Man, thank you guys so much. If it weren't for this place, I probably would have lost my apartment because all my money would have gone to food instead of rent. It's helped me get by for these past five months as I've been searching for work.

Lile continued to tell us about the profound impact the shopping program has had on people's lives,

> I've heard a lot of similar stories of people just saying thanks. It's not the typical image a lot of us have of people on welfare. It's often people who have just fallen on hard times because of the economic downturn and they needed that little extra boost. What I love to see is sometimes the people that are in line serving and hosting the guests jump out of line because their number gets called and now they're going through the line because they need a little help, too.

Lile also told us about Brandon, an auto mechanic.

Brandon is the one of the top mechanics in Akron, Ohio. Brandon experiences the creativity of God in working on vehicles, seeing how intricate they are and how wonderfully they're made. And he senses the brokenness of the world because he's constantly working on broken things! Yet he is painfully aware that, as a blue-collar worker, he doesn't always get the respect extended to people in white-collar professions. And Brandon knows that people only come to him when there's a problem. Yet I've seen Brandon really affirmed in his position. Brandon was promoted to the role of shop foreman and has had opportunities to change the culture of his workplace. Formerly employees walked around the garage with their heads down. Now people walk with their heads high, a transformation achieved in part by affirming the work that they do. As Brandon felt his work affirmed, he, in turn, affirmed the work of others.

Newer churches like City Hope Church are not the only ones seeking partners to do outreach and missions. More established churches like Christ Community Church in Kansas City, Missouri, also see the value of partnering with like-minded friends. To that end, Christ Community has teamed up with Christ Fellowship Baptist Church, located in the urban core of the city. Nelson says that faith, work, and economic wisdom theology played a pivotal role in the partnership from the beginning. This is wise because for many churches located in underserved urban areas, economic justice and economic equality are central concerns. Outreach and missions for Christ Community Church has involved hosting a conference with the theme of pursuing "Common Good" for the wider Kansas City metropolitan area.

When we asked Nelson to share a story of someone deeply impacted by the theology of faith and work, he recounted the story of a business leader.

This business owner was designing his corporate headquarters. During the design phase he and his leaders started to think through not only how to treat their employees, but also the spaces in which they would work. In particular, he thought through how his faith would shape the workplace itself and its design. He's deeply invested in a seamless faith, in his family. He wants to create a virtuous company with fair and equal policies and practices. But he's asking, 'How does my faith speak into my corporate headquarters in terms of the architectural space, structure, and how it's designed?' He's allowing the gospel to speak into every aspect of his life, personal and professional.

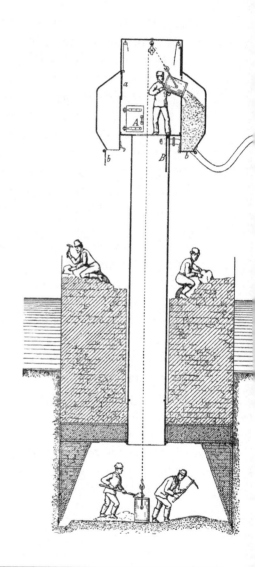

NONPROFITS CAN MAKE IT LESS COMPLICATED

Many pastors found that an effective way to promote faith and work integration was by starting a nonprofit. For example, in Woodlawn, located on the Southside of Chicago, Brad Beier told us the unemployment rate is about 23 percent. So, as Beier led an effort to restore an old dilapidated building — formerly an old pool hall for hustling, prostitution, and drugs (that would later serve as the worship center) — where people off the streets were invited to do meaningful work. Beier said that their mantra was, "If you want money, or if you want help, we will give you work to do." It became apparent that one of the best ways to serve their neighborhood was by giving people meaningful work. Seeing the promising results of this initiative, Beier then started a nonprofit economic development ministry called Hope Works.

Hope Works is focused on economic empowerment. It serves as an on-ramp for participation in the ministry, relationship-building, and discipleship. Striving to give people good, dignifying work has not been without its challenges. Many people off the street expect cash after working and not a paper check. However, they're seeing promising results. Beier recounted a story about a young man who has been with him for four years. The man did construction work for about six months before visiting the church and is now a member. Another worker was dating a woman at the church but was also hustling and selling drugs. He was hired after visiting the church and continued coming. Eventually he was baptized and joined the church. On Father's Day of that same year, this man said, "I can't believe that I am celebrating Father's Day in a church with my family! I was hustling and selling drugs and you got me pounding nails and sweating and getting dirty and doing hard work. It's really difficult, but I'm enjoying it now."

Living Hope Church (and Hope Works) is establishing a reputation on the Southside of Chicago. Once, some college students were asked to canvas the neighborhood and hand out flyers. When they returned, Beier asked them how it went. They reported hearing comments like this from neighbors: "I got a job through Hope Works." Another guy said, "Oh yeah, that's my church, and they helped me with my employment."

Pastor Stan Archie and Christian Fellowship Baptist Church created an organization called the Community Impact Center. This center works with homeless male veterans and increasingly with female veterans. Partnering with Hope Faith Ministries of downtown Kansas City, they work with homeless people who struggle with drug and alcohol addictions. Recently, Community Impact Center staff have identified and targeted neighborhood laundromats as a focal point of their efforts in the community. There they pay for people's laundry and listen to their stories to assess how the church can serve them in concrete ways. With great excitement, Archie said, "Down the road they want to launch an urban version of Made to Flourish!"

Living Hope and Christian Fellowship Baptist Church remind me of something that Reading of United Evangelical Free

Church said at the beginning of our interview: "Quit trying to be the best church in the city that competes with other churches. Be the best church for the city, so that if you were to shut your doors, the city would mourn." That's a good mandate for any church. Is your church competing, or are you striving to be the best church for the city?

A CAFÉ: FROM PRISON-TO-WORK TRAINING GROUND

Joe Tucker is executive director of a nonprofit known as South Street Ministries. South Street runs a community restaurant called The Front Porch Café. This café is located one block from the Summit County Jail. "We're one block from a couple of other institutions that house inmates. And we're also in a neighborhood that was a local hub for a lot of recovery meetings," he told us in an interview.

Many of the workers at the café, in fact, come from backgrounds of incarceration, addiction, or poverty. Having workers with such backgrounds has been quite helpful; they're adept at distinguishing fact from fiction. "Running such a ministry," Tucker says, "takes discernment." He explains, "So, a café staff member may say to a patron, 'Hey, man, this one is on us today. And since you're having a rough day, let's sit down and talk. Here's some eggs and toast.' However, if someone steps through our threshold and says, 'Hey, I'm looking for something to eat. I need something,' the conversation may go like this to discern if the person is a hustler or if the person genuinely needs assistance:

Café staff: "Sorry, we don't give money out loosely. If we don't know who you are, you could be hustling us. Would you help us clean the restroom for a bit today? And then we can get you a meal afterwards."

Patron: "No, I'm good today. I'll go somewhere else."

Café staff: "Okay, I guess you weren't that hungry after all."

Tucker said they have a lot of those interactions, and often they are preceded or followed by prayer. A lot of folks frequent the café enough that they know what's going on. "That's the ministry philosophy behind it," explained Tucker. "This practice separates the wheat from the chaff. It shows which folks are really ready to do the right thing versus the ones looking for a quick fix or quick money."

Sometimes Tucker and the staff will allow people to volunteer for a season for a variety of reasons. For example, the café has folks who volunteered to get a job reference. For someone like this, a café staff member might say, "Volunteer at the café for a few days. We'll give you meals, and you can take tips home. If you're a good worker, we'll write you a good reference."

Tucker added, "If we don't have a reference point for your workmanship, we won't recommend you to an employer. So often volunteering at the café is a test." Doing volunteer work is a great opportunity to see if the worker will show up on time and demonstrate integrity. It can also lead to gainful employment elsewhere.

The café's philosophy is working. The success has created a "good problem." They routinely lose their best employees because they move on to better jobs. Tucker and others were acutely aware of this problem when suddenly the food stopped being as good as it was before! The café, as a result, has had to tweak its philosophy and practice a bit to keep some of these dutiful workers. However, they still make room for people in need of work. "If someone crosses the café threshold and is just really trying to look for a job and discouraged," Tucker said, they will "help them out with that process." Still sometimes patrons just use the café as a public restroom, or for the public phone, or to use their tables to write their cardboard signs. "Regardless, the cafe staff will love on them," he said.

ENTREPRENEURSHIP: WALKING WITH THE OLD AND YOUNG

Many churches are addressing the "E" in FWE by coming alongside and assisting those interested in being entrepreneurs. For instance, Mullins' past work includes an entrepreneurship initiative with the Uzbek refugee community. He connected entrepreneurs from his church with refugee entrepreneurs to help start new businesses. The goal was for these startups to financially support the refugee entrepreneurs and their families. This effort was supplemented by providing English and citizenship classes.

Pastor Ward is a pastor at Abundant Life Church and also teaches entrepreneurship courses at Gordon Conwell Theological Seminary in Boston, Massachusetts. From one class, 40 businesses were proposed and 30 of those 40 are still vibrant and contributing to their respective communities. To help maintain that vibrancy, Ward and other mentors meet with these entrepreneurs every quarter.

At Abundant Life, in place of the traditional VBS, Ward's church sponsored a *BIZ* Camp. Here, young people, like his son, were taught how to develop business plans. Seasoned business leaders served as "sounding boards" to help these aspiring teenage entrepreneurs fine-tune their business plans and, eventually, launch new businesses. Ward's son's small business was so successful that he put the vending machines at his school out of business.

Tabernacle Community Church sponsored The Youth Entrepreneur Leadership Program. In this program, middle school students were exposed to entrepreneurship teaching for seven weeks during the summer.

Pastor Lindsay wanted to show these students that God has called us to be creators and to reflect his image as a creator. During the summer, these students developed business plans and presented them to local entrepreneurs in a *Shark Tank* style environment.

Although missions and outreach is the least developed area at Jefferson Assembly of God Church, pastor Duncan is beginning to think about bringing small business development into some economically depressed neighborhoods. This is especially needed because people with limited resources, such as an unreliable vehicle, must drive 20 miles or more just to get to work. The church has also been looking at a program called Strengthen Families to help family units in these depressed areas. Duncan envisions using the principles in Steve Corbett and Brian Fikkert's book, *When Helping Hurts*, to foster far-reaching, long-term change.

COMMUNITY ENGAGEMENT AND BEYOND

For the last four years, Fernando Tamara has hosted a prayer breakfast where he has invited local religious leaders to meet and dialogue with civic leaders. To date, sheriffs, food bank executives, legislators, financial consultants, and the chief of police have addressed and eaten with these religious leaders. He also invites local organizations that champion economic innovation like Southern California Edison (an electric company that provides power to homes), the Center for Sustainable Energy, Thrivent Financial, and Bread for the World.

Tamara takes community engagement a step further by serving as a chaperone for 12-15 pastors as he travels with them to Washington, D.C. on Bread for the World's Lobby Day. Here, these pastors learn how a bill becomes a law and how to conduct themselves in the company of a legislator. Once home, Tamara serves as a mentor to these pastors by helping them engage with and interpret American politics.

Pastor Gail Roberts-House and Open Door Full Gospel Baptist Church have adopted a local elementary school where kids have to wear uniforms. According to the school's family engagement specialist, kids often come to school in dirty uniforms. So Roberts-House and her church plan to buy the school a washer and dryer. In addition to this gesture, Roberts-House and Open

Door plan to launch and oversee self-reliance boys and girls clubs for fifth graders at the school. Boys and girls will make products such as pottery, bracelets, Lego-transformers and sell these products at PTO meetings and school carnivals. A local credit union has pledged to cover the cost of the supplies. Roberts-House hopes that these students will learn the joys and challenges of being entrepreneurs, and the biggest lesson that God has gifted them with gifts and potential. In the words of Roberts-House, "We want these students to form a legacy" of self-reliance rather than an unhealthy dependence.

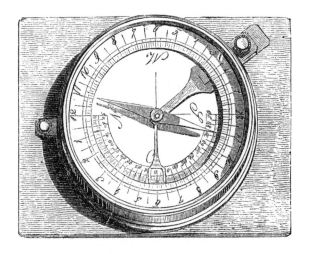

Conclusion

Infusing FWE theology into the life of the church can be frustratingly slow, but it is often rewarding. Pastors interviewed have spoken of their "awakening" to this important theology and are prayerfully seeking ways to integrate this theology into four areas in their local bodies: pastoral practices, the corporate worship gathering, discipleship/spiritual formation, and mission/outreach.

Some of their efforts have been met with success, while other efforts have not. Much of the progress, thus far, has come in the areas of corporate worship and pastoral practice. Most churches interviewed confessed that integration of FWE theology in the areas of discipleship/spiritual formation and outreach have been slow. However, this is not because they don't deem these areas important; sometimes the reason for the slower progress is limited manpower, bandwidth, or knowledge on how to proceed. Nonetheless, we hope that this sampling of churches that are helping their congregants see discipleship as an all-of-life affair will inspire you. As you've met pastors and congregations on the pages of this book that are helping their people connect Sunday to Monday, we hope it has sparked imaginative ideas that will help you implement a similar vision in your local church context.

Acknowledgments

We are grateful for our partners in this work, Denise Daniels (Seattle Pacific University), Mark Roberts (Max De Pree Center for Leadership, Fuller Theological Seminary), and Chris Armstrong (Kern Family Foundation), who all did a careful reading of this second edition manuscript. We believe this second edition is far better with their reviews and comments.

ABOUT THE AUTHORS

SKYE JETHANI is an award-winning author, speaker, and ordained pastor. He served as both the managing and senior editor of *Leadership Journal* and as the director of mission advancement for *Christianity Today*. He currently co-hosts *The Phil Vischer* Podcast. Because of his diverse cultural upbringing and training in religious pluralism, Skye has been a sought-after voice for groups facing challenges at the intersection of faith and culture, including The Lausanne Movement and The White House Office of Faith-Based and Neighborhood Partnerships. Skye has written for many publications including *Relevant* and *The Washington Post*, and he is a regular contributor to *The Huffington Post*. Skye is ordained with the Christian & Missionary Alliance and has served as a pastor in Wheaton, Illinois. He is a "Featured Preacher" on *PreachingToday.com*, and he speaks regularly at churches, conferences, and colleges in the U.S. and internationally including Q, Catalyst, Mars Hill Bible Church, and the U.S. Naval Academy. Skye has authored six books. His latest writing project is *With God Daily*, a subscription-based daily devotional that helps thousands in the smartphone generation begin their day with God.

LUKE BOBO serves as director of strategic partnerships for Made to Flourish and brings a rich blend of experience to the organization, having worked for 15 years as an electrical engineer before pursuing an M.Div. and Ph.D., and eventually serving as the executive director of the Francis Schaeffer Institute at Covenant Seminary. Luke has spent time as a professor of religious studies at Lindenwood University and currently works as an adjunct professor of contemporary culture and apologetics at Covenant Seminary. In addition to writing curriculum for a workplace ministry, Luke has written *Living Salty and Light-filled Lives in the Workplace*, *A Layperson's Guide to Biblical Interpretation: A Means to Know the Personal God*, and *Race, Economics, and Apologetics: Is There a Connection?* Luke has lectured and preached in Cape Town, South Africa and Goiania, Brazil. He currently serves as the minister of Christian education at Friendship Baptist Church, Kansas City, Missouri.

APPENDIX: BOOKS MOST CITED BY INTERVIEWEES

Dennis Bakke. *Joy at Work: A Revolutionary Approach to Fun on the Job*. Seattle, WA: PVG, 2005.

Craig G. Bartholomew and Michael W. Goheen. *The Drama of Scripture: Finding Our Place in the Biblical Story*. Grand Rapids, MI: Baker Academic, 2004.

Drew Cleveland and Greg Forster (Eds.). *Pastor's Guide to Fruitful Work & Economic Wisdom: Understanding What Your People Do All Day*. Waukesha, WI: Made to Flourish, 2014.

Steve Corbett and Brian Fikkert. *When Helping Hurts*. Chicago, IL: Moody Publishers, 2009.

Andy Crouch. *Culture Making: Recovering our Creative Calling*. Downers Grove, IL: IVP, 2008.

Steve Garber. *Visions of Vocation: Common Grace for the Common Good*. Downers Grove, IL: IVP, 2014.

Os Guinness. *The Call: Finding and Fulfilling the Central Purpose of Your Life*. Nashville: Word Publishing, 1998.

I, Pencil. Article. www.econlib.org/library/Essays/rdPncl1.html.

Tim Keller and Kathryn Leary Alsdorf. *Every Good Endeavor: Connecting Your Work to God's Work*. New York: Dutton, 2012.

Tom Nelson. *Work Matters: Connecting Sunday Worship to Monday Work*. Wheaton, IL: Crossway, 2011.

Dorothy Sayers. "Why Work". In *Letters to a Diminished Church: Passionate Arguments for the Relevance of Christian Doctrine*. Nashville, TN: W Pub. Group, 2004.

Dorothy Sayers. "Creed or Chaos". In *Letters to a Diminished Church: Passionate Arguments for the Relevance of Christian Doctrine*. Nashville, TN: W Pub. Group, 2004.

Amy Sherman. *Kingdom Calling: Vocational Stewardship for the Common Good*. Downers Grove, IL: IVP, 2011.

Gene Veith. *God at Work: Your Christian Vocation in All of Life*. Wheaton, IL: Crossway, 2002.

Bruce Winter. *Seek the Welfare of the City: Christians as Benefactors and Citizens*. Grand Rapids, MI: Eerdmans,1994.

Christopher J. H. Wright. *The Mission of God: Unlocking the Bible's Grand Narrative*. Downers Grove, IL: IVP Academic, 2006.

Christopher J. H. Wright. *The Mission of God's People: A Biblical Theology of the Church's Mission*. Grand Rapids, MI: Zondervan, 2010.

N. T. Wright. *Surprised by Hope: Rethinking Heaven, the Resurrection, and the Mission of the Church*. New York: HarperOne, 2008.

ENDNOTES

1 See https://www.theologyofwork.org/.

2 Nathan Miller Tweet, July 20, 2016.

3 Freddy Williams and David Comstock, Story Catechism, 51.

4 FLOW, produced by Acton University, stands For the Life of the World. This accessible seven-episode video/digital series uses the prophet Jeremiah's letter to the exiles in Jeremiah 29 as a launching pad to instruct us what it means to live as "exiles" in our contemporary context. Perhaps the most insightful episode is the one on "Creative Service." Here the FLOW creators demonstrate beautifully how our work, a creative service and an economic activity, contributes to a mysterious, enormous, and organic collaboration with others for the sake of the life of the world.

5 "Work as Worship" is part of a DVD series with Matt Chandler, Norm Miller, and J.R. Vassar. It was produced by RightNow Media and is available online at RightNowMedia.org.

6 The Gotham program was started at Redeemer Presbyterian Church in New York and is now replicated in cities across the country through the Redeemer City to City Network. This program is a leadership development pathway designed to integrate faith and work. This program requires commitment: it is a nine-month intensive course and costs $2,200. The program combines heavy theological training with real-life integration. Fellows are assigned daily readings and are required to give up two hours a week, one Saturday a month, and three weekends per year. Yet their program's rigor has not scared off applicants. Rather, the demand continues to grow. They have had over 100 applicants every year. For more information, see http://faithandwork.com/programs/1-gotham-fellowship.

7 For more information, see https://denverinstitute.org/5280-fellowship.

8 For more about Surge, see http://surgenetwork.com.

9 See Work: The Meaning of Your Life by Lester DeKoster.

My Notes

Made in the USA
Monee, IL
18 July 2021